Funnier Bone Jokes

Funny Valentine's Day JOKES to Tickle Your FUNNY BONE

Linda Bozzo

Enslow Elementary

an imprint of

Enslow Publishers, Inc.

40 Industrial Road
Box 398
Berkeley Heights, NJ 07922
USA

http://www.enslow.com

Enslow Elementary, an imprint of Enslow Publishers, Inc.

Enslow Elementary® is a registered trademark of Enslow Publishers, Inc.

Library of Congress Cataloging-in-Publication Data

   Bozzo, Linda.
   Funny Valentine's Day jokes to tickle your funny bone / by Linda Bozzo.
       p. cm. — (Funnier bone jokes)
   Includes index.
   Summary: "Read jokes, limericks, tongue twisters, and knock-knock jokes about Valentine's Day.
Also find out fun facts about the holiday"—Provided by publisher.
   ISBN 978-0-7660-4119-6
   1. Valentine's Day—Juvenile humor. I. Title.
   PN6231.S16B69 2013
   818'.602—dc23
                         2012007703

Future editions:
Paperback ISBN 978-1-4644-0177-0
ePUB ISBN 978-1-4645-1090-8
PDF ISBN 978-1-4646-1090-5

Printed in the United States of America

082012 Lake Book Manufacturing, Inc., Melrose Park, IL

10 9 8 7 6 5 4 3 2 1

To Our Readers: We have done our best to make sure all Internet Addresses in this book were active and appropriate when we went to press. However, the author and the publisher have no control over and assume no liability for the material available on those Internet sites or on other Web sites they may link to. Any comments or suggestions can be sent by e-mail to comments@enslow.com or to the address on the back cover.

Every effort has been made to locate all copyright holders of material used in this book. If any errors or omissions have occurred, corrections will be made in future editions of this book.

♻ Enslow Publishers, Inc., is committed to printing our books on recycled paper. The paper in every book contains 10% to 30% post-consumer waste (PCW). The cover board on the outside of each book contains 100% PCW. Our goal is to do our part to help young people and the environment too!

Illustration Credits: Clipart.com, p. 1, 6 (left), 7 (middle), 12 (bottom), 13 (top), 16, 18, 19 (bottom), 21 (bottom), 22 (bottom), 23 (bottom), 27 (top), 30 (bottom), 32 (top left), 37 (bottom), 38 (bottom), 39 (right), 40, 42 (top), 43 (top), 44 (top); Photos.com, p. 15 (top); Photos.com: art12321, p. 34 (bottom), Christos Georghiou, p. 4 (bottom), Cruz Puga, p. 15 (bottom), Dmitriy Kolesnikov, p. 29 (middle), Dynamic Graphics, pp. 21 (top), 41 (middle), 43 (top), Eleonora Ivanova, p. 28, fractal, p. 10 (bottom), Iryna Vanina, p. 14 (bottom), Iurii Lupol, p. 11 (top), James Lee, p. 36 (bottom), Jana Guothova, p. 31 (bottom), Jennet Chua, pp. 31 (middle), 37 (top), John Rawsterne, p. 33 (bottom), Kathryn Swezy, p. 20 (top), KathrynAnnSwezy, p. 38 (top), Kenn Wislander, p. 33 (middle), Klara Viskova, p. 9 (bottom), Laura Analía Taira, p. 24 (top), Len Neighbors, p. 30 (middle), len_pri, p. 33 (top), Leo Blanchette, p. 22 (top), Maria Bell, p. 19 (top), Philip Boyd, p. 6 (right), Z-Art, p. 20 (bottom); Shutterstock.com, pp. 4 (top), 5, 6 (top), 7 (top, bottom), 8, 9 (top, middle), 10 (top, middle), 11 (bottom), 12 (top, middle), 13 (bottom), 14 (top), 17, 20 (bottom), 21 (middle), 23 (top 3), 24 (bottom), 25, 26, 27 (middle, bottom), 29 (top, bottom), 30 (top), 31 (top), 32 (top right, bottom), 34 (top), 35, 36 (top, middle), 39 (left, bottom) 41 (top, bottom), 42 (bottom), 44 (bottom).

Cover Illustration: Shutterstock.com

Contents

The History of Valentine's Day

Knock, knock.

Who's there?

Tail.

Tail who?

Tail all your friends it's Valentine's Day.

Merry maids marry on Mondays.

What did one porcupine say to the other?

I'm stuck on you.

What did one insect say to the other?

Bee my sweetheart.

BEE MINE!

DID YOU KNOW?

Did you know that some people believe Valentine's Day started with the ancient Roman feast of Lupercalia? It's true! Named after the Roman god Lupercus, the feast was celebrated from February 13 through February 15. Young girls would write their names on pieces of paper and place them in a vase. Each boy would choose a name from the vase. The girl he chose would be his partner for the festival and maybe even the year. These matches would often turn into love and sometimes even marriage.

DID YOU KNOW?

Many countries around the world celebrate love with family and friends on Valentine's Day. In the United States, Valentine's Day is February 14.

What did the boy snake say to the girl snake on Valentine's Day?

"Give me a hug and a hiss, honey."

If Maria married Harry and Larry married Mary, then who married Mabel?

How did the elephant and the ant start dating?

It began as a crush.

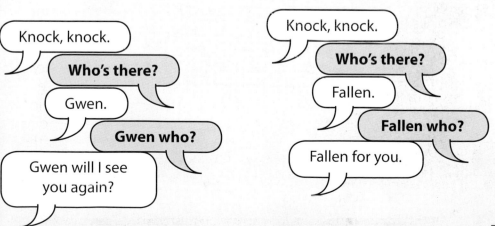

Knock, knock.

Who's there?

Gwen.

Gwen who?

Gwen will I see you again?

Knock, knock.

Who's there?

Fallen.

Fallen who?

Fallen for you.

DID YOU KNOW?

Did you know that Valentine's Day is named after a priest named Valentine? It's true! Long ago, the ruler of Rome believed married men did not make good soldiers. To keep his soldiers in shape, he would not allow them to get married. Valentine did not think this rule was fair. It was said that Valentine married young lovers in secret. When the ruler found out, he put Valentine in jail and had him killed. Valentine was buried on February 14, and later he was declared to be a saint. That is why, each year on this day, people celebrate St. Valentine and love.

Limerick

There were two lovers from Redding.
Plenty of tears they were shedding.
When their parents found out
It was onions no doubt,
They let them go through with their wedding.

Knock, knock.

Who's there?

Weed.

Weed who?

Weed like to get married someday.

What did the farmer give his wife for Valentine's Day?

Hogs and kisses.

There was a young man named Sid
Who loved a poor girl named Mid,
But her awful smell
They couldn't dispel,
and even the skunks ran and hid.

Miss Mary may marry Mister Harry in March or May.

BE MINE

There once was a boy named Chris
Who longed to have just one kiss.
He joined in the game,
And pulled out a name,
And said, "Who in the world is this?"

What did the octopus say to his girlfriend on Valentine's Day?

What did the boy owl say to the girl owl on Valentine's Day?

"I want to hold your hand, hand, hand, hand, hand, hand, hand, hand."

"Owl be yours."

I Love You!

Is it better to write "I love you" on a full stomach or an empty stomach?

It's better to write it on paper.

Knock knock.

Who's there?

Olive.

Olive who?

Olive you.

There was a gentleman so kind
He had just three words on his mind.
He took out his pen
And time and again
"I love you," he signed and he signed.

Why do skunks celebrate Valentine's Day?

They're very scent-imental.

FUN FACT

Did you know *"Te quiero"* means "I love you"? It's true! It's what you might say to a friend in Spanish. You could also say, *"Ti amo"* (tee ah-moh)—and the same phrase would work in Italy. What about someone in France? You would say, *"Je t'aime"* (zhuh tehm). To someone in Germany, you would say, *"Ich liebe dich"* (ikh lee-beh dikh).

What did one light bulb say to the other light bulb?

" I love you a watt."

What did the ram say to his sweetheart?

I love ewe.

What did the boy elephant say to the girl elephant?

"I love you a ton."

Lola's lazy leopard living in London loves to lick lots of lemons.

A Labradoodle named Blue
Chewed on his favorite shoe.
He'd whisper and then
He'd say it again,
"I love you. I love you, my dear shoe."

Little Lizzy loved Dizzy
Lizard's love letters better.

Knock, knock.

Who's there?

Tail.

Tail who?

Tail everybody I love you.

What did one oar say to the other oar?

"Can I interest you in a little row-mance?"

DID YOU KNOW?

A love seat is a double chair or small sofa that is just big enough for two people. Did you know that love seats were not originally designed for two people to sit on? It's true. In the late seventeenth and eighteenth centuries, these wide chairs were made for just one person to sit. The larger size was to allow more space for the large dresses of the time period. In the nineteenth century, these chairs became known as courting chairs.

❸ Hearts

Nurse: Can I take your pulse?

Boy: Why, haven't you got one of your own?

What did one slice of bread say to the other?

"I loaf you with all my heart."

DID YOU KNOW?

Hearts are a common symbol of Valentine's Day. People like to decorate their classrooms and homes with hearts. The heart is actually a muscle that pumps blood through your body. But did you know that human heart does not look much like a valentine heart? It looks more like a muscle and weighs less than one pound. It's true!

FUN FACT

A long time ago, people thought their feelings came from their hearts. But did you know your emotions really come from your brain? That's right. It is actually the brain that tells the heart when to beat faster. The human heart beats about 100,000 times a day. Did you know that women's hearts beat faster than men's hearts?

What did the painter say to her boyfriend?

"I love you with all my art."

Harold's healthy heart hardly hurries.

Limerick

There was a blond boy named Bart
Who drew a nice girl a heart.
She loved it and said,
"I think we should wed."
And Bart cried, "What did I start?"

There was a young man named Pete
Whose heart had a very fast beat.
But when his new bride
Stood next to his side,
Her heart beat faster than Pete's.

Knock, knock.

Who's there?

Blake.

Blake who?

Blake my heart.

What did the father say to his son on Valentine's Day?

"We need to talk heart to heart."

Knock, knock.

Who's there?

Heart.

Heart who?

Heart it was Valentine's Day.

How many beats must a human heart beat before the blood reaches the feet?

15

What two words have a thousand letters in them?

Post office.

Viola's very violet valentines vanished.

What do you call a very small valentine?

A valentiny.

Knock, knock.

Who's there?

Eye.

Eye who?

Eye know who gave me this valentine.

What did the letter say to the stamp?

"You send me."

DID YOU KNOW?

Do you know the legend of the valentine? It is thought that long ago, a man named Valentine sent the first valentine greeting. He may have fallen in love with a young blind girl who visited him while he was in prison. Some say Valentine helped cure a blind girl. Before he was killed it is said that he wrote the girl a letter and signed it, "From your Valentine." These words are still used today.

What did the stamp say to the envelope?

"I'm stuck on you."

How does a werewolf send his valentines?

By hair-mail.

Pam packed plenty of pretty purple paper.

FUN FACT

Charles, the French Duke of Orleans, sent the first and oldest known written valentine to his wife. It was a love letter that included a poem. This valentine, from 1415, is on display at the British Museum.

Knock, knock.

Who's there?

Anita.

Anita who?

Anita piece of paper to make a valentine.

Limerick

There once was a girl all undone.
Of Valentine cards she had none.
Then her dog came along
With a dance and a song
And gave her the funniest one.

A silly young man left his meeting
To buy an unusual greeting.
He opened the card
And thought very hard,
Then decided it wasn't worth keeping.

Seven stacks of stamps stuck to my size six pants.

What did the ice cream do when it got a valentine?

It melted.

ROSES ARE RED...

FUN FACT

The first Valentine's Day greeting cards made in the United States were created by Esther A. Howland in the 1840s. After receiving her first valentine from England, she became interested in making cards herself. She was the first person to start a business selling valentines in the United States. She created fancy cards using lace, flowers, and ribbons. That is why she is known as the Mother of the Valentine.

5 Valentine Celebrations

Why is Valentine's Day the best day for a celebration?

Because you can party hearty.

Limerick

There once was a girl named Marty
Who thought she was such a smarty.
She called twenty gals,
Who each brought three pals
And made it a valentine's party.

FUN FACT

Not everyone celebrates Valentine's Day the same way. For instance, did you know that in Japan, the women buy chocolate for the men on February 14? One month later, on March 14, the men give chocolate to the women. In Great Britain, people celebrate by writing poems for their loved ones. At one time, British children went door to door in groups, singing valentine songs.

21

Knock, knock.

Who's there?

Bacon.

Bacon who?

Bacon cupcakes for the party.

Corey cuts cute cupid cookies with the cupid cookie cutter.

Kid: Dad, why do I have to go to the Valentine's Day party?

Dad: Because the party won't come to you

Charlie chews cherry chocolate chip cupcakes carefully.

Who keeps track of the cookies you eat?

The kitchen counter.

Limerick

There once was a girl from Love Lake
Who decided to bake a cake.
It looked like a heart,
But it fell apart.
Her cake was declared a mistake.

DID YOU KNOW?

Did you know that Valentine's Day wasn't always celebrated in the United States? It's true. For many years, Valentine's Day was celebrated only in Rome. When Roman soldiers fought in other countries, like England, they brought their Valentine's Day traditions with them. Americans received valentines from their friends in England before the tradition came to the United States. Today, Valentine's Day is celebrated not only in Rome, but in countries all around the world.

Limerick

There are lots of valentine treats,
A table of drinks and sweets.
We all play fun games,
They call out our names,
And everyone gets to eat!

Parker picks Patty to pass a piece of party pizza.

Cupid

What did the girl say to the cupid?

"You make me quiver."

Knock, knock.

Who's there?

Thumb.

Thumb who?

Thumb body saw Cupid.

Sue saw Cupid shoot six singing arrows at her sister Sharon.

DID YOU KNOW?

Did you know that long ago, the people of Rome believed Cupid was the god of love? It's true! Old Roman stories told that his mother was Venus, the goddess of love, and his father was Mercury, the messenger god. This is probably why stories of Cupid say he delivered love to others.

How did Cupid get to the Valentine's Day party?

He followed the arrows.

What does Cupid put on all of his Valentine's Day presents?

Bows and arrows.

Which white wings will William want to wear Wednesday?

Why did the horse think she was getting married?

She had a bridle fitting.

What do cherubs serve at their parties?

Angel food cake.

Limerick
There was a lady from Dresser
Whose love grew lesser and lesser
For a man named Ted,
Whom she thought she'd wed,
But he just got fresher and fresher.

25

FUN FACT

Cupid has long been a part of Valentine's Day celebrations. He is known as a young child with wings who is full of mischief. He carries a bow and arrows of love. Did you ever wonder why Cupid is a symbol of Valentine's Day? In stories from long ago, he used his bow and arrows to shoot the hearts of people. This would cause them to fall madly in love with the next person they saw.

Limerick

There was a cupid with wings
Who did some talented things,
But words he could not
Remember a lot
For all of the songs he sings.

How did Cupid go to visit his mother in Florida?

On an arrow-plane.

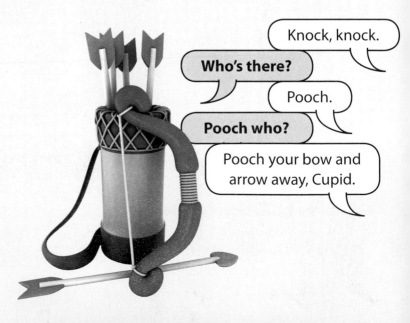

Knock, knock.

Who's there?

Pooch.

Pooch who?

Pooch your bow and arrow away, Cupid.

A cupid who liked to fly
Just couldn't understand why
Two lovers had fought,
Which gave him the thought:
I'll try them again in July.

Knock, knock.

Who's there?

Warren.

Warren who?

Warren earth
is Cupid?

What happened when two angels got married?

They lived harp-ily ever after.

Why did the two ghosts get married?

It was love at first fright.

Valentine Chocolates

How did you pass the entrance exam to get into candy-making school?

It was easy, I fudged it.

What did one chocolate heart say to the other?

Will you be my sweet-heart?

Knock, knock.

Who's there?

Don't chew.

Don't chew who?

Don't chew know I love chocolate?

Limerick

There was a closet of sweets,
Left over from trick-or-treats.
On Valentine's Day,
Joe threw them away.
Now fruit is all that he eats.

DID YOU KNOW?

Many people give chocolate treats to their friends and family for Valentine's Day. The Hershey's plant in Hershey, Pennsylvania, makes many different kinds of chocolate products. Did you know that the Original Hershey's Kisses Brand Milk Chocolates were introduced in 1907? It's true!

Why didn't the hermit crab share his candy?

Because he was shell-fish.

Why don't they serve chocolate in prison?

So the prisoners won't break out.

Knock, knock.

Who's there?

Weirdo.

Weirdo who?

Weirdo you get your chocolates?

Silly Shari shares six cherries with her serious sisters Sharon and Mary.

Limerick

There was a lady who made
Chocolate wherever she stayed.
People complained,
"Oh, what a shame,
She gave all the chocolate away!"

Knock, knock.

Who's there?

Howard.

Howard who?

Howard you like a five-pound box of chocolates?

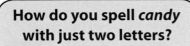

How do you spell *candy* with just two letters?

C and Y.

Nick's shop shipped chopped chocolate-dipped donuts.

What do aliens like to eat with their chocolate?

Martian-mallows.

FUN FACT

Some chocolate candies have a sweet filling in them. Did you know that two people from Switzerland made this possible? In 1912, Swiss-born Jean Neuhaus invented the chocolate shell. These shells could be filled with creams and nuts. Then in 1913, Jules Sechaud invented the first chocolate-filling machine. This made filled chocolate less expensive. Thanks to both of these inventors, people can get their fill of filled chocolates for Valentine's Day.

Why did the pig give his girlfriend a box of candy?

Because it was Valen-swine-day.

What's the best thing to put into a chocolate candy?

Your teeth.

Limerick

There once was girl named Mandy
Who liked to eat too much candy.
Her head would shake,
Her stomach would ache,
So her bed came in quite handy.

8 Flowers and Teddy Bears

What did the bee say to the rose?

"Hi, Bud."

Knock, knock.

Who's there?

Tanks.

Tanks who?

Tanks for the beautiful roses!

Why do bears have fur coats?

Because they would look funny in denim jackets.

Two dozen fancy fresh flowers froze.

DID YOU KNOW?

When it comes to flowers, roses are the most popular to give on Valentine's Day. Red roses have long been thought of as a symbol of love. Did you know that in November 1986, President Ronald Reagan made the rose the National Floral Emblem of the United States?

Where do roses sleep?

In flower beds.

What does a teddy bear put in his house?

Fur-niture.

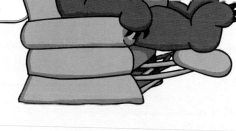

Limerick

There was a young boy who felt bad
That his girlfriend was feeling so sad,
So he gave her a flower,
And in just one hour,
She was feeling gladder than glad.

What kind of flowers kiss on Valentine's day?

Two-lips.

Limerick

A dozen roses or more
Were left in front of my door.
Within two hours
There were no flowers
And petals covered the floor.

Knock, knock.

Who's there?

Vick.

Vick who?

Vick some flowers for me?

How do you start a teddy bear race?

"Ready, teddy, go!"

FUN FACT

In addition to flowers, chocolates and teddy bears are popular Valentine's Day gifts. Did you know that the teddy bear is named after President Theodore Roosevelt? The president, whose nickname was Teddy, had been on a bear-hunting trip. No bears could be found. Near the end of the trip someone finally caught a bear. President Roosevelt refused to shoot it. It was a cartoon of this event that inspired a toy bear named Teddy's Bear. It's true!

Knock, knock.

Who's there?

Arthur.

Arthur who?

Arthur any flowers at the store?

Flowers r Us

Three bees sneezed then wheezed before whizzing up to the trees.

⑨ Lovebirds

You know what they say about a bird in hand?

It poops on your wrist.

What did the parrot say when he saw the duck?

"Polly want a quacker?"

What's a parrot's favorite game?

Hide and speak.

Why did the bird join the air force?

It wanted to be a parrot-trooper.

Baby birds burp worms.

DID YOU KNOW?

Lovebirds are known as a symbol of Valentine's Day. Do you know why? It's probably because these birds will spend their lives with the same mate. These colorful birds belong to the parrot family. They are often seen in pairs, spending a lot of time together. That is why people who are in love or who are always together are called "lovebirds." Stories from long ago say that lovebirds choose their mates on February 14.

Knock, knock.

Who's there?

Alf.

Alf who?

Alf feed the birds.

What do you get if you cross a parrot with a bee?

A bird that is always telling you how busy he is.

Large lazy lovebirds like little literature lessons.

Knock, knock.

Who's there?

Chicken.

Chicken who?

Chicken out the lovebirds.

Limerick

There was a bird named Nate
Who couldn't find a mate.
He searched at night
And thought he might—
But then it got too late!

What's the difference between a fly and a bird?

A bird can fly but a fly can't bird.

Limerick

There once was a young lovebird
And though you may not have heard
The bird would sing
The same ol' thing
For he only knew one word!

Knock, knock.

Who's there?

June.

June who?

June know two lovebirds?

FUN FACT

A female lovebird is called a hen. When hens are around six months old, they are ready for mating. They will usually lay between 4 and 6 eggs over 4 to 6 days. It takes about 23 days for the hen's eggs to hatch. But the eggs won't all hatch at the same time. They will hatch in the same order that the hen laid them, about a day apart. The young lovebirds won't open their eyes for at least 10 days. It's true!

Little Lisa loves lovely little lovebirds.

How does a parrot with a broken wing land safely?

With a parrot-chute.

What do you call two birds in love?

Tweet hearts.

I LOVE YOU

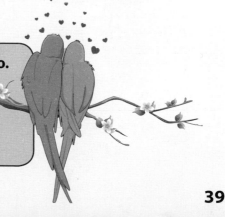

Limerick

Lovebirds, snuggling, there are two.
Oddly, both of them are Lou.
They look the same
And it's a shame—
I can't tell which Lou is who.

Kooky Connie claps for cool clever calendar colors.

Knock, knock.

Who's there?

Butter.

Butter who?

Butter wear red today.

When do kangaroos propose?

On leap day.

What makes a calendar so popular?

It has lots of dates.

DID YOU KNOW?

Valentine's Day isn't the only U.S. holiday in February. There's Groundhog Day on February 2, which lets people know whether winter will last another six weeks. Presidents' Day celebrates the birthdays of Abraham Lincoln and George Washington on the Monday between the two. Mardi Gras, or Fat Tuesday, is a celebration of feasting and fun. It falls before Ash Wednesday, the beginning of the more serious season of Lent. The Super Bowl is a football game played on the first Sunday in February. The winning team is that season's national football champion. While Super Bowl Sunday isn't really a holiday, many people across the country celebrate it.

Why was the calendar so scared?

Its days were numbered.

Farmer Frank feels February flies past fairly fast.

Limerick

There was a fellow named Ted
Who on the fourteenth did wed
The love of his life
who now is his wife.
"I do, I do," they both said.

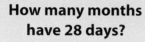

How many months have 28 days?

All of them.

What does a guy who loves his car do on February 14?

He gives it a valen-shine.

FUN FACT

Have you ever wondered why the color red is a symbol for the month of February? Red is the color of blood that is pumped through people's hearts. Hearts have long been a symbol of love and Valentine's Day. Today, red valentine hearts are used to decorate homes and classrooms for Valentine's Day. Many people wear red clothing or clothing with hearts on it for Valentine's Day. So would it surprise you to know that February is also American Heart Month?

BE HEART SMART
American Heart Month

Limerick

When February comes around
Soft wet snow will cover the ground.
We slip and we slide
Until we decide
We're tired of falling down.

Make Your Own Funny Valentine

HERE'S WHAT YOU WILL NEED:

- A joke book

- A piece of construction paper

- Markers or crayons

- Other decorations, such as stickers, stamps, and pieces of wrapping paper (optional)

DIRECTIONS:

1. Choose one of the jokes or limericks in this book.

2. Fold the construction paper in half like a card.

3. Write the beginning of the joke or limerick on the front of the card.

4. Write the punch line on the inside of the card. If you use a limerick, write the last line on the inside of the card.

5. Use markers to illustrate the joke.

6. You can use other decorations, such as stickers, stamps, or even cutouts from wrapping paper, to make the card more special.

7. Remember to write on the back of the card, "Handmade by (your name)."

8. Finally, write your own special message to the person—just as you would on a store-bought card.

Words to Know

ancient—Long ago.

Cupid—The Roman god of love.

feast—A very large meal, usually shared by a lot of people.

joke—Something that is said to make you laugh.

limerick—A funny poem that is usually five lines, where lines 1, 2, and 5 rhyme, and lines 3 and 4 rhyme.

lovebird—A type of parrot. Lovebirds generally live in pairs, and they often snuggle cheek to cheek.

mate—To become a couple; to come together to make little ones.

symbol—Something that stands for something else.

tongue twister—Fun words that when put together can be hard to say.

tradition—A belief or custom handed down over the years.

valentine—A card to show friendship or love.

Read More

Books

Dahl, Michael, Kathi Wagner, Aubrey Wagner, and
Aileen Weintraub. *The Everything Kids' Giant Book of
Jokes, Riddles & Brain Teasers*. Avon, MA:
F + W Media, 2010.

Leno, Jay. *How to Be the Funniest Kid in the Whole World
(or Just in Your Class)*. New York: Aladdin Paperbacks,
Simon & Schuster Children's Publishing, 2007.

Phillips, Bob. *Super Incredible Knock-Knock Jokes for
Kids*. Eugene, OR: Harvest House Publishers, 2007.

Internet Addresses

Giggle Poetry
<http://www.gigglepoetry.com/>

Jokes & Humor—Yahoo! Kids
<http://kids.yahoo.com/jokes>

Jokes By Kids
<http://www.jokesbykids.com>

Index